GW00792783

The
Evangelists

by
J. B. Midgley

*All booklets are published thanks to the
generous support of the members of the
Catholic Truth Society*

CATHOLIC TRUTH SOCIETY
PUBLISHERS TO THE HOLY SEE

Contents

Acknowledgements

The Catholic Truth Society gratefully acknowledges recourse to the following sources. *The Psalms, Grail Translation*, Catholic Truth Society, London, 2003. *Catholic Dictionary*, Virtue and Co. Ltd, London, 1951. *Catholic Encyclopaedia*, The Encyclopaedia Press, London, 1907. *The Lost Bible*, J. Porter, Duncan Baird, London, 2003. *Catechism of the Catholic Church*, Geoffrey Chapman, London, 1993. *The Jerusalem Bible*, Darton, Longman & Todd, London, 1974. *The Divine Office*, Collins, London, 1974. *The Complete Bible Handbook*, J. Bowker, Dorling Kindersley, London, 1998. *Catholic Commentary on the Holy Scripture*, Thomas Nelson & Sons, London 1951. *Papal Documents*, Catholic Truth Society, London. *History of Christianity*, Owen Chadwick, Weidenfeld and Nicolson, London 1995. *Eusebius of Caesarea* (translations), G. A. Williamson, Harmondsworth, London 1965.

Unable to live on bread alone

Matthew, Mark, Luke, and John offer loving and powerful friendship to all who proclaim the Good News of the Kingdom by the way they live, and support those given the specific mission to preach the Gospel.

As the third millennium began, Pope John Paul II reminded the world that it depends not only on bread but also on the Word of God "who wishes to be seen and heard in the gentle person of His Son whom we can rediscover in the Gospel." He later added that "the preaching of the Gospel has disseminated and consolidated values which have given European culture a global influence, and the Church, with renewed sense of responsibility, is eager to preserve this patrimony and revitalise Europe's Christian roots."

The Archbishop of Westminster has called for a confident commitment to tell the world about the Kingdom of God, and recommended meditation upon "the Gospel's relevance in the daily tasks of life in a deep relationship with Christ who teaches us in parables." The Bishops of England and Wales have reiterated that this is the time for Christians to proclaim the Gospel with renewed confidence, conscious of their Baptismal call to continue the Apostolic mission to make disciples of all nations in the name of the Holy Trinity.

In his first encyclical, *'God is Love'*, Pope Benedict XVI concludes that "the lives of the saints are not limited to their earthly biographies, but continue being and working in God after death. They do not withdraw from men, but rather become truly close to them. Like the Blessed Virgin Mary, they love every generation with a benevolence that results from intimate union with God, through which the soul is totally pervaded by Him, a condition which enables those who have drunk from the fountains of God's love to become, in their turn, a fountain from which 'flow rivers of living water.'"

May this booklet bring us into closer contact with these four great evangelists.

Downham Market, Lent 2007

The Good News

Our Lord "came to Nazareth where He had been brought up, and went into the synagogue... He stood to read, and they handed him the scroll of the prophet Isaiah. Unrolling the scroll He found the place where it is written, 'The Spirit of the Lord has been given to me, for He has anointed me. He has sent me to bring the Good News to the poor, to proclaim liberty to captives, and to the blind new sight, to set the downtrodden free, to proclaim the Lord's year of favour'" when all debts are cancelled. He explained that this was central to His ministry: "I must proclaim the Good News of the Kingdom of God... because that is what I was sent to do." He delegates this same mission to His disciples through the ages, "Go out to the whole world: proclaim the Good News to all creation." So Isaiah's prophecy is fulfilled: "How beautiful on the mountains are the feet of one who brings the good news, who heralds peace, brings happiness, proclaims salvation, and tells Zion, 'Your God is King.'" (*Is* 52:7, 61:1-2, *Lk* 4:16-19, 42-43).

The Kingdom of God

"The Kingdom of God is most visible in Christ, the Son of God and Son of Man who came to serve and give His life as a ransom for many... When He rose again after suffering death on the Cross for mankind, He made clear that He had been appointed Lord, Messiah, and Priest forever, and breathed on His disciples the Spirit promised by the Father. Since Pentecost, the Church is entrusted with the task of announcing and extending the Kingdom here on earth. Equipped with her Founder's gifts, and faithfully guarding His precepts of charity, humility, and self-sacrifice, she receives the mission to proclaim and establish among all peoples the Kingdom of God, and strive towards its glorious consummation with her King" (*'Dogmatic Constitution on the Church'* 5, 1965, abridged).

Proclaiming the Good News

On the Feast of the Immaculate Conception, 1975, Pope Paul VI issued his Apostolic Exhortation *'On Proclaiming the Gospel in the Modern World'*. In what has been considered his most important pronouncement, he associated evangelisation with the Church's concern for the well being of society. She proclaims the coming of the reign of God as "liberation from sin and the Evil One... and from economic, social and political oppression." He added that, while it is of the essence of the Church's mission to evangelise, she must begin "by being evangelised herself" (*'Evangelii Nuntiandi'* n.9, 15, 29).

The Evangelist

The description comes from the Greek meaning "the one who proclaims good news". In the New Testament, disciples like St Timothy and St Philip the Deacon are included among all who are called evangelists because they bring the Good News of God's Kingdom to others, and form a group so important that St Paul lists them among God's gifts to the Church after Apostles and Prophets. The Twelve Apostles appointed by Our Lord are not the only missionaries identified in the Gospels. There are, for example, the "seventy-two" whose mission St Luke describes in detail, the devoted women "who accompanied the Lord from Galilee and supported His brethren", and a further group that included the scribe Joseph of Arimathaea.

In his commentary on the Gospel of St John, St Cyril of Alexandria writes that "Our Lord Jesus Christ appointed certain men to be guides and teachers to the world and stewards of His divine mysteries... to light up, as do the sun, moon and stars, and to shine not only on the country of the Jews, but on every country under the sun and on all men who dwell upon the earth. He called His disciples before all other men to the glorious apostolic office, and to be the pillar and ground of the truth, for Christ said He had sent them just as the Father had sent Him. Thus He showed both the dignity of their apostolic office and the incomparable glory of the power transmitted to them, and suggested the manner of life they should follow. He explained the purpose of their office when He told them that He had come to call sinners to repentance, and to do the will of the Father who had sent Him to save the world. As He sends them, they must understand their duty to call sinners to repentance, to heal the afflicted, whether in the body or in the spirit, and in all their conduct of affairs to seek not their own will but the will of Him who had sent them and, insofar as His teaching was now theirs, to save the world" (cf. *Lk* 6:12-16).

Model of Mary

The Most Blessed Virgin Mary is the luminous example of discipleship in her response to God's call and her role in the history of salvation. She is mother to all God's people whose discipleship she protects. She is the figure of the Church, and Queen of those whom her Son asks to preach the good news of the Kingdom. The evangelising mission of the Apostles and their successors is the activity of the Church that Our Lord has established as the sacrament of God's people from Adam until the end of time. She is the flock which knows and is known, loves and is loved, and is the new Jerusalem. She is the high-walled holy city whose twelve gates open to reveal His Father's loving intentions from the moment He called

Abraham until His Son comes again in glory to present the perfected Kingdom planned from all eternity. "The Lord comes to gather the nations of every language... As an offering to the Lord they will bring all to the holy mountain in Jerusalem, and some who seemed so far away are raised up as priests and Levites" (*Is* 66:18-21; *Ps* 84; *Rv* 12:1, 21:9-14).

Interpretation, literary forms

In the third century St Hippolytus and Tertullian initiated the practice of honouring Saints Matthew, Mark, Luke and John, as the Four Evangelists and writers of the canonical Gospels chosen by God to record, with the inspiration of the Holy Spirit, the truth He wishes to impart for our salvation. Since He speaks through human beings, scriptural interpretation benefits from an examination of writers' methods of presenting what has been revealed so that the audience can understand. In 1943, Pope Pius XII explained that the correct "literal" sense of the Scriptures is understood in the context of the "literary" forms and expressions used at the time they were written. When, for example St Mark says that Our Lord spoke to His listeners "only in parables", he refers to a familiar teaching method. In other circumstances, Our Lord enjoyed conversations with people from every walk of life and had a special appeal to children who are demanding judges of character. Similarly, St John presents Our Lord's "I am" metaphors: the "Bread of Life... Light of the World... Good Shepherd and Gate of the Sheepfold...The Resurrection and the Life...Way, the Truth and the Life...True Vine." While historical exegesis helps contemporary readers comprehend ancient texts, care must be taken not to have too easy a recourse to figurative and allegorical explanations, especially if the meaning seems harsh and demanding. The Pope recommended prayerful study of the Scriptures, reliance on the traditional teachings of the Church, and trust in the guidance of the Magisterium. (cf. *Mk* 4:34; *Jn* 6:28-15:17; Encyclical *'Divino Afflante Spiritu'*, 'Inspired by the Holy Spirit').

Historical validity

The Church approves the historical validity of the Gospels and teaches that they faithfully transmit what Our Lord said and did for our eternal salvation until the day He ascended to His Father. After the coming of the Holy Spirit at Pentecost, the Apostles had a deeper understanding of the events of His life and were able to teach by the light of the Spirit of Truth. The Evangelists selected from what had been communicated by word of mouth in society, and "wrote from their own memory and recollections, and from the witness of those who 'from the beginning were eyewitnesses and ministers of the word, so that we could know the truth of what they had learned.'"

St Jerome says that, in order to preserve the Gospel whole and alive in the Church, the Apostles appointed bishops to inherit their teaching role, a sacred tradition that is like a mirror in which the pilgrim Church looks at God from whom she has received everything until she finally sees Him as He is, face to face (*Lk* 1:2-4; 1 *Jn* 3:2; *Dogmatic Constitution on Divine Revelatio*n 7, 1965).

Four Gospels: the same Good News

The Gospels of Matthew, Mark and Luke are of similar character and content, and their accounts of Our Lord's life, ministry, and death can be read in parallel. Consequently, they are called Synoptics from the Greek *'Synopsis'* meaning "things that can be seen with the one eye." Gospels are announced "according to..." the individual Evangelist to whom authorship is ascribed because they are not four Gospels, but four expressions of the same Good News about Our Lord's character, what He says and does, and His teaching. They also reveal how preachers captured the interest of the early Christians by sharing with them the memories of His first, personal followers. The Sermon on the Mount and the Parables, for example, are arranged to facilitate teaching, learning, and convey the truth of what He says with love. John's Gospel, written later in the first century, retains the structure of the Synoptics, but is a more meditative reflection on the significance of Our Lord's words and deeds, and retains the historical tradition that links the missions of St John the Baptist and Our Lord.

Symbols

Later reference will be made to St John's vision in the Book of Revelation of God who entrusts the future of the world to the Lamb and His Evangelists whose symbols were first recognised by St Irenaeus of Lyons. "Grouped around His Throne were four animals with many eyes, in front and behind. The first was like a lion (Mark), the second like a bull (Luke), the third had a human face (Matthew), and the fourth was like a flying eagle (John). Each had six wings and eyes all the way round, and day and night they never stopped singing, 'Holy, Holy, Holy is the Lord God Almighty: He was, He is, and He is to come'" (*Rv* 4:7). Historians continue to discuss theories of authorship by a single person or by an anonymous Christian group that assembled oral teachings under a chosen name. Suffice it to say that the Church honours Matthew, Mark, Luke and John as the inspired writers of the Gospels. The number of lines devoted to each is no indication of rank, and differs only by the inclusion of selected themes and the range of individual activities.

Saint Matthew

Capernaum and taxation

A small fishing settlement on the northwest shore of the
Sea of Galilee grew to be the first significant place
reached after crossing the Jordan frontier from the east. It
was a convenient rendezvous for the pilgrims who joined
caravans on their way to Jerusalem for the Pasch and
other Feasts, and it benefited from the trade routes linking
Egypt, Mesopotamia, Damascus, Arabia, and Gaza that
followed a north easterly direction through Galilee. It was
the hometown of Peter's wife, and they moved here from
Bethsaida after their wedding. His brother Andrew
followed, and James and John became regular visitors.
Our Lord was a frequent guest and so fond of the place
that He made it a second home. It was here He taught in
the synagogue, promised the Eucharist, and healed many
people including Peter's mother-in-law whose recovery
was so instant that she rose from her sickbed and cooked
them all a meal.

The Romans developed Capernaum as a military port
and provincial seat of government with a garrison
commanded by a centurion whose main task was to
supervise the collection of taxes, especially the lucrative

toll-charges and revenues from the fishing industry. Roman officials found tax collection distasteful and beneath their dignity, so they contracted the task out to the highest bidders, the "publicans" who appear in the Gospel. These not only collaborated with the occupying power; they extorted tax at a rate higher than required so that there was a tidy surplus for their own pockets after paying the franchise fee. They even enlisted military assistance to enforce demands so that, all in all, they were heartily loathed by the Jews who classified them as sinners, outcasts from society, and ritually unclean.

"Follow me!"

It was inevitable that Our Lord should know that Matthew was the area tax collector, but astonishing that He should speak to him, let alone call him to be a disciple. Even those who already followed Him would have been disgusted at the way publicans lined their own pockets at the expense of others, especially the poor, but Jesus shows that God's love for every individual is indiscriminate, unconditional and constant. In His Kingdom all are welcome to the grace the Gospel brings, and the socially, physically and religiously marginalized are embraced as eagerly within His family as those who might seem more favourably qualified. On another occasion, another wealthy tax collector, Zacchaeus, was so moved by Jesus' wish to be his guest, so transformed by the contact, that he gave half his goods to the poor and compensated those he had cheated.

Matthew recalls how Our Lord invited him to become a follower, and his immediate response to His magnetism. "As Jesus was walking (in Capernaum), He saw a man named Matthew sitting by the customs house, and He said to him, 'Follow me.' And he got up and followed Him." This abrupt abandonment of the customs house and a financially rosy future, is a powerful example of the rejection of money that became an ideal for early Christians who regarded wealth as for sharing, not keeping. As tax collectors were tools of Roman occupation, this was also something of a political as well as a spiritual conversion (*Mt* 9:9).

Eating with sinners

The amazed and delighted Matthew asked Our Lord to a celebration dinner, an invitation more significant than it would be today because, in accepting, Jesus was ignoring religious and social protocol, and acknowledging Matthew as a close friend and part of a family circle. This kind of meal was something of a public spectacle, and Pharisees watched from the open doorway. They were furious at Our Lord's presence, especially since Matthew had also invited his equally "sinful" friends and business colleagues. However, despite their offended rabbinical sensitivities, they did not think the time was ripe to attack Jesus directly, so they berated his disciples instead: "Why does your master eat with tax collectors and sinners?"

Our Lord heard them and said, "It is not the healthy who need the doctor but the sick. Go and learn the meaning of the words: 'What I want is mercy, not sacrifice.' And indeed I did not come to call the virtuous, but sinners," indicating that God would prefer to have real, interior devotion to outward observance of the Law. His words are more telling, and His conduct in accord with God's mind, because it was a mere Pharisaic practice and not the Law that forbade eating with publicans, sinners and Gentiles. Sinners and outcasts are made in God's image and have an intrinsic holiness waiting to flower, and they become saints through the amazing effect He has on their lives. The professional religious leaders did not realise that His power is made perfect in infirmity, that it is sinners whom He calls to repentance, not those who are so confident about their own virtue that they feel no need for the mercy that transcends ritual sacrifice. This is the only time Matthew receives individual attention in the New Testament, but what an occasion it is.

Disciple and martyr

When he lists the Apostles in his Gospel, he is not ashamed of his name or profession, and calls himself "Matthew the tax collector", letting everyone know that Our Lord includes the most unlikely candidates in discipleship. When Mark and Luke speak of his vocation, they identify him as "Levi, son of Alphaeus", perhaps from delicate consideration, though it was common Hebrew practice to have two names. When they speak of the Twelve, however, they call him Matthew, a name that means "gift of Yahweh" (cf. *Mt* 9:9, 10:3; *Mk* 2:13-14; *Lk* 6:15 5:27-32, 6:15)

As with other Apostles, tradition fills the gaps left by history about what happened to Matthew after Our Lord's Ascension. He is said to have taken the Gospel to the Middle East and, according to Epiphanius, fourth century bishop of Cyprus, he was martyred while preaching in Hierapolis in Parthia, now part of Turkey. The Roman Martyrology says this happened while he was preaching in Ethiopia but, according to the 'Martyrology of Jerome', he gave his life in Tarsuana, east of the Persian Gulf. It is believed that his relics were brought first to Brittany from Ethiopia, and then translated to Salerno in Sicily in the eleventh century by Robert Guiscard.

Matthew's Gospel

Matthew's Gospel achieved a special prominence at the beginning of the second century thanks to St Clement and St Ignatius of Antioch, and no alternative author is mentioned. Later, St Irenaeus, Eusebius and Origen agreed that Matthew preached to the Hebrews, and wrote a Gospel in their own language of such precision and style that it is ideal for reading to an audience. His main theme is that Christ brings the reign and Kingdom of God that, in Him and through Him, remains with His Church until the end of time. He begins with the story of the Infancy and concludes with the Passion, the account of which is similar to Mark's but adds some miraculous occurrences that demonstrate the reality and extraordinary nature of the Resurrection and Ascension.

The five discourses

While generally following Mark's outline of events, he uses the revered structure of the five Mosaic Books to arrange material in five discourses that he begins with a narrative to draw fuller attention to Our Lord's teaching:

1. The Sermon on the Mount and Our Lord's moral teaching (*Mt* 5-7)
2. His visionary message as He sends His Apostles on their mission (*Mt* 10)
3. His teaching in Parables (*Mt* 13)
4. His code of Christian behaviour, and view on Matrimony *(Mt* 18-19)
5. The last days and the coming of the Kingdom (*Mt* 24-25)

Towards the end of the first century AD, there was tension between Jewish and Gentile converts to Christianity. Matthew opens his Gospel with the "genealogy of Jesus Christ, son of David, son of Abraham," to assure every one that Jesus is indeed the Messiah whose coming was foretold by the Prophets, and that He is the fulfilment of God's promise to the Patriarch's of the Jews and, through them, to all the nations. He tells of the Magi's visit when the Divine Infant reveals Himself to all the peoples of the earth, an Epiphany that in no way neglects Jewish heritage and Law, but completes the Scriptures so that God's Law is for all, Jews and Gentiles alike. (cf. *Mt* 28:19)

The Scriptures have foretold the life and ministry of Jesus, the incomparable Rabbi who now introduces Himself in the Sermon on the Mount, the introductory charter of the Kingdom of God. Later, Matthew mentions the role of the Church and its authority to teach, legislate, and make disciplinary decisions, but so that there is no moral and religious discord, he urges her to be merciful in judgement with childlike humility. Our Lord asks disciples to obey His teaching because neither the Old Law nor His words will pass away and God's divine plan is not to be thwarted. (cf. *Mt* 16:18-19, 18:1-18, 21:4, 24:35, 27:9,35).

Our Father: the Lord's Prayer

The awesome picture of the Old Covenant's 'Most High', gives way to the Kingdom of His love that was there all the time but is now in hearts open to receive it. Matthew took for granted that the Jewish converts for whom he wrote, were familiar with the traditional method of prayer, but both he and St Luke wanted to tell their respective Jewish and Gentile audiences that there was no shame in finding prayer difficult.

Even the disciples who had spent so much time with Our Lord asked for His guidance. He tells them, "In your prayers, do not babble as the pagans do, for they think that by using many words, they will make themselves heard. Do not be like them; your Father knows what you need before you ask Him, so you should pray like this: "Our Father, who art in Heaven, hallowed be thy Name, thy Kingdom come, thy will be done on earth as it is in Heaven. Give us this day our daily bread, and forgive us our trespasses as we forgive those who trespass against us. And lead us not into temptation, but deliver us from evil." (*Mt* 6: 7-13)

St Cyprian (200-258) recognises the prayer's perfection and power: "For the benefit of our salvation, Our Lord has guided us in our life of prayer. He who has given us life teaches us how to pray with the same kindness He shows in His other gifts. When we pray to the Father He delights to hear us use the words His Son has given us. Our prayer is friendly and intimate when we petition God with the Son's own prayer, letting His words rise to the Father's ears. He who dwells in our breast is our voice, our advocate who joins us in pleading forgiveness for our sins. He said, 'Whatever you ask the Father in my name, He will give it to you.' It follows that we shall certainly obtain what we want if we use the words that the Father recognises as His Son's. He shows us that prayer is an honest, uncomplicated reflection of what is felt in the heart, rather than a recitation of things because they seem appropriate. He entrusts to His disciples the fundamental Christian prayer that is at the centre of the Scriptures, and is a summary of the Gospel. It is the 'Lord's Prayer' because it is composed by the Lord Himself, God the Son, who is the Master and Model of all prayer."

"Heaven" is our Father's House, His majestic presence in human hearts, and the Homeland where we belong. We share in His divine plan by praying that every person and nation will sanctify the Name that He revealed to Moses and Jesus. The Church prays for its growth here on earth, and looks forward eagerly to when Our Lord comes again to present the perfected Kingdom to His Father. We ask the Father to unite our will to His Son's so that the plan of salvation comes to fruition in the world.

Hallowed be thy name

"When we say, 'hallowed be thy name', we ask that it should be hallowed in us who are in Him, and in others whom God's grace still awaits. We ask that we may obey the precept that obliges us to pray for everyone, even our enemies, and that is why we do not say 'hallowed be thy name' in us, for we ask that it be so in all" (Tertullian).

"We ask God to hallow His name which by its own holiness saves and makes holy all creation and gives salvation to a lost world. We ask that it becomes holy in us through our actions, for His name is blessed when we live well, but is blasphemed when we live wickedly." (St Peter Chrysologus)

"Thy Kingdom come" is the desire that God will reign in our hearts in this world and, through His grace, bring us to His heavenly home. Present sorrow is outshone by future glory as Baptism washes sin away, and creation is born again in the Holy Spirit to reign with Him forever. In the meantime the Kingdom is interdependent with the work of the Church in the world as she seeks to advance the Kingdom in every personal and social context, proclaiming Christ's teaching of the Kingdom and the Good News that it has arrived in human hearts. Hers is not a political programme looking for a social Utopia, though she is not indifferent to situations that are alien to God's reign.

Thy will be done

"'Thy will be done' asks the Holy Spirit for help to co-operate in the Father's plan, as did Mary, the Angels and Saints who now proclaim His glory as they enjoy His vision. Obedience to His will enlarges the exercise of freedom that recognises the potential disasters of human inclination to less desirable choices, and accepts that the One who created us individually understands what is good for us more clearly than we do ourselves, for His Law is perfect, 'is to be trusted and gladdens the heart'" (cf. *'Pastoral Constitution on the Church in the World of Today'*, 39)

In communion with all members of the human family we trust the Father to give us the daily bread we need for our body's subsistence, and the Bread of Life, the Body of Christ who is the Word of God for our soul's nourishment. In His eternal present, this Eucharist is a joyous anticipation of the Banquet in the heavenly Kingdom and, with the "Our Father", is the perfect prayerful anticipation of His Second Coming at the end of time with salvation complete.

We ask God to forgive our sins, and let His mercy penetrate our hearts so that we forgive those who offend us, following the example of Our Lord who is always there with His support. Then, to show our love for God, we ask Him to help us avoid the tempting paths that can lead to offending Him, and to give us the grace to be vigilant and faithful to the end.

Temptation

"Lead us not into temptation" is the only petition expressed negatively. God is not prone to temptation Himself and does not tempt anyone else, but we ask Him to help us resist the temptations that come our way as a result of the Fall. We know from St Paul that God never allows anyone to be tempted beyond his strength, and every temptation comes with an escape route. Sometimes God might give us an opportunity to show a particular virtue that edifies and encourages others, as He did with Abraham and Job for example, but this is not temptation. (*Gn* 22; *Jb* 1; 1 *Co* 10:13).

"Deliver us from evil" is a plea that we will not succumb to the power of evil that attacks us in the form of temptation to sin, to be rid of Satan who "goes round like a roaring lion seeking whom he may devour." St Augustine views this as a request for general relief from sin, sickness, afflictions, misfortunes, and evil in general. St Thomas Aquinas prefers to think of God delivering us from evil by giving the comfort without which we could not endure. He compensates us for afflictions with His consoling blessings, and turns trials and afflictions to our advantage as we are inspired by the Holy Spirit to pray for deliverance from Satan's attacks while we wait patiently for the happiness of heaven (cf. 1 *P* 5:8).

The problem of evil

The Church begins the Communion Rite of the Mass with the Lord's Prayer. She asks the Father for release from the past, present, and future evils that Satan instigates, and for peace and perseverance as she awaits the return of His

Son. "Deliver us Lord from every evil and grant us peace in our day. In your mercy keep us free from sin and protect us from all anxiety as we wait in joyful hope for the coming of our Saviour, Jesus Christ."

God is infinitely good, and the universe He created is likewise good. His Son has redeemed us once and for all and, in the light of eternity, the struggle between good and evil is over. The world of time, however, is still beset by temptations, plagues, wars, inhumanity, suffering, and death, the present evils that God tolerates in the achievement of salvation. In the person of Adam, the human race copied Satan and his followers by rejecting the chance to show love for the Creator, and the created order was wounded by this first, representative sin of disobedience that characterised all subsequent decisions to ignore God's Law.

At the root of sin is a freely made decision to place personal inclination before the worship we owe Him. In the moral context, the dignity we share with the angels to make free choices can have unwanted results. God does not offend our freedom by preventing wrong choices, but He does not remain aloof from our self-imposed predicament, nor does He want us to suffer retribution. His continuing providence realises His plan of salvation through freedom, not coercion, and His merciful remedy is that all are saved from the consequences of sin through faith in Jesus Christ.

His incarnate Son has adopted wounded human nature that now shares in His divinity, and He has repaid all our debts. As the source of sanctifying grace, He restores our integral union with the Father and shows us how to resist Satan by His own victory over temptation in the wilderness. The prophets' expectations are wonderfully fulfilled: "The blind see, the lame walk, the lepers are cleansed, the deaf hear, the dead are raised to life, and the good news is proclaimed to the poor." Despite the world's sorrows, there is a glorious expectation, and "happy is the man who does not lose faith in Him." His atonement restores the supernatural order, ends the slavery of sin and, in the union of His Mystical Body and infinite merits, He gives the grace to face life's trials, and conquer the powers of darkness. (cf. *Mt* 4:1-11, 11:1-6; *Is* 35:1-10).

The blind and the lame and are still among us, and we are all subject to suffering and death. This does not mean that the mission of Our Lord's first coming is incomplete, but that the healing miracles He accomplished as Saviour await the perfection of His second coming. "Christ, having been offered once to bear the sins of many, will appear a second time, not to deal with sin but to save those who are eagerly waiting for Him." Then, "everlasting joy shall be upon their heads... and sorrow and sighing shall flee away." This final victory over evil is proclaimed at the end of the New Testament: "He will wipe away every tear from their eyes, and death shall be no more, neither shall there be mourning nor crying nor pain any more, for the former things have passed away." (*Is* 35:10; *Heb* 9:28; *Rv* 21:4).

Devotion to St Matthew

"Lord, you showed great mercy to Matthew the tax gatherer by calling him to become your Apostle. Supported by his prayer and example may we always answer your call, and live in close union with you" (*Prayer of the Church*).

"It is not surprising that the tax collector should leave the earthly gains he was looking after at the first command of the Lord and that, abandoning riches, he should join the company of Him he saw had no wealth. For the Lord who outwardly called him with words, through a hidden instinct secretly taught him to follow Him. By the gift of divine grace, the Lord enlightened his mind to understand that He, who on earth called him away from temporal interests, could give incorruptible treasures in heaven" (St Bede the Venerable, *Office of Readings*, September 21st).

St Matthew is the patron of the diocese of Salerno where his relics are enshrined in the cathedral church dedicated to him. In art he is represented both as Apostle and Evangelist, holding an inkwell, or writing the Gospel at his desk with an angel guiding his hand. In representations dating from the Middle Ages, he wears reading glasses, sometimes holding a moneybag as a reminder of his tax gathering days, or with the sword, spear, and halberd that were the instruments of his martyrdom. One of Matthew's emblems as an Evangelist is a human being (*Rv* 4:7), the male figure of the genealogy that reveals the Messiah's descent from the house and lineage of David, as the prophets had foretold, and His membership of the human family.

During the papacies of Popes Pius XII and Paul VI, curial decrees declared St Matthew the patron of accountants, bankers, tax collectors and customs officers. The West celebrates the Feast of St Matthew, Apostle and Evangelist on September 21st, and the East on November 16th. As recently as August 2005, a group of Bible experts and archaeologists reported they had found the ruins of an ancient monastery in the central Asian state of Kyrgyzstan where, according to tradition, the saint was initially buried.

Saint Mark

In the New Testament, the Evangelist is known as John Mark or Mark. Jews in the Roman Empire often had two names, so there is nothing unusual in the Roman 'Marcus' being added to the Hebrew 'John'.

"Having been delivered from prison, Peter went to the house of Mary, the mother of John Mark" (*Ac* 12:12).

"Aristarchus who is here in prison with me sends his greetings, and so does Mark, the cousin of Barnabas... if he comes to you give him a warm welcome" (*Col* 4:10).

"Get Mark to bring Luke to you. I find him a most useful helper in my work" (2 *T* 4:11).

"Epaphras... sends his greetings; so do my colleagues Mark, Demas and Luke" (*Phm* 24).

St Peter writing from Rome refers to "my son Mark" and says that he is his interpreter. (1 *P* 5:13).

Mark's house

Mark's mother Mary was a prominent member of the infant Church in Jerusalem, and her house was a meeting place and haven for the disciples. When Our Lord needed an upper room where He could celebrate the Passover with the Apostles, it was to her that Peter and

John went because she was one of the many householders in the city who rented accommodation to pilgrims arriving for the great feasts. When Our Lord was arrested in the Garden of Gethsemane, "a young man who had followed Him had nothing on but a linen cloth." They caught hold of him, but he left the cloth in their hands and ran away naked." As Mark is the only Evangelist to mention this incident, it seems he was writing about himself. Tradition dating from the second century also includes him as one of the seventy-two disciples sent out by Our Lord. About 41 AD, when Peter escaped from prison with the help of an angel, his first sanctuary was the house of Mark and his mother (cf. *Mk* 14:51-52; *Lk* 22:7-13; *Ac* 12:12).

Missionary work

Meanwhile, the Christians in Antioch sent Paul and Barnabas, Mark's cousin, to Jerusalem with alms for the relief of the poor who were suffering from the famine that had overtaken the city. When they returned to Antioch to resume the first missionary journey (38-48 AD), Mark went with them preaching the Good News in Cyprus and onwards to Perga in Pamphilia. For some unknown reason, he did accompany them to Turkey but returned to Jerusalem, much to Paul's annoyance. When the second missionary journey was being planned in Antioch, Barnabas suggested that Mark should remain one of the team, but Paul refused because he had not completed the first journey. After a further difference of opinion about the appropriate form of table-fellowship between Jewish and Gentile Christians, Paul chose Silas to accompany him on the mission to Syria, Cilicia, and Macedonia in 49 AD. Mark returned to Cyprus to join Barnabas who established the Church there and, according to Tertullian, contributed to the *Letter to the Hebrews*. Any residual ill feeling soon evaporated, and Paul expressed his appreciation of Mark's collaboration and contribution in his letters to Philemon and Timothy, and commended him to the Colossians' hospitality. (cf. *Ac* 11:29, 13:5,13, 15:36-41).

Rome

About 54 AD, Mark went to Rome and became the companion and interpreter of Peter who provided him with material for his Gospel. At the time, Christianity was tolerated, even appreciated, and there were conversions in every level of society, but things changed with Nero's persecution. Christians in the provinces were naturally anxious about the dangers and sufferings experienced by their brothers and sisters in the capital. In his first letter, Peter writes to encourage them not to waver, and says how much he values the support of his "son Mark". The paternal remark is not only affectionate but may well indicate that, as a family friend, he had baptised him.

Since he sends greetings from Mark to the Christians of Pontus, Galatia, Cappadocia, Asia, and Bythinia, it seems they knew him well because he had played his part in their evangelisation.

Eygypt

According to St Jerome and Eusebius, Mark could not have been in Rome continuously because he took Christianity to Egypt and founded the Church in Alexandria where he was the first bishop. Eusebius says he passed responsibility for the See of Alexandria to Ananias in 62 AD and rejoined Peter and Paul in Rome. He was certainly there when Peter wrote his letters, and when Paul contacted Timothy about 64 AD. The apocryphal *Acts of Mark* and the *Paschal Chronicle* record that after the deaths of Peter and Paul he returned to Alexandria where he suffered martyrdom at the hands of marauding Arabs in 74 AD (cf. *Ac* 11:27-30, 12:12-25, 13:13; 1 *P* 5:13; *Eccl. Hist.* 20.16:1-2; 2:24).

Mark's Gospel

The early Christian tradition that ascribes authorship to Mark is exemplified by Eusebius, the father of church history, who quotes Papias: "John the Presbyter, (either St John the Apostle, or another contemporary disciple), says that Mark wrote accurately what he remembered of the things said and done by the Lord. He was a follower of Peter who instructed as circumstances demanded, though not necessarily in chronological order. Mark was concerned to record the truth and omit nothing that he had heard." (Papias: bishop in Asia c. 120 AD, prominent church elder, historian, friend and collaborator of St Polycarp who was a disciple of St John).

St Clement and St Jerome tell us that Mark put St Peter's oral catechesis into writing more for the benefit of Christians in Rome than for Jewish Christians. He explains Jewish customs only to assist his listeners, identifies Jordan as a river, Mount Olivet as being near the Temple, and the Parasceve as the day before the Sabbath. Generally, he omits details that a Jewish audience would have found unnecessary, and does not dwell on the Mosaic Law, the fulfilment of Old Covenant prophecies, or the denunciation of scribes and Pharisees. He refers to the "Kingdom of God" unlike Matthew whose sensitivity to his Jewish audience prompted him to speak of the "Kingdom of Heaven." "Yahweh" was a name so sacred to the Jews that it was uttered only once a year, and then by a priest officiating at a Temple ceremony and, fearful of using God's name inappropriately, they preferred "Adonai", "Lord." No doubt thanks to Peter, Mark is able to depict scenes with particular realism and eyewitness details, for instance the cure of the paralytic, the generosity of the impoverished widow who gives her last penny to the

Temple treasury, and the vivid description of Our Lord in the stern of the boat, "His head on a cushion, asleep," just before He calms the storm on the Sea of Galilee (*Mk* 2:1-12, 4:38, 12:42).

First to be written

Though second in the canonical order, there is wide academic conviction that Mark's Gospel was the first to be written and that Matthew and Luke found it an admirable framework and source of information about Our Lord's person and mission, to which they added further details from a collection of recorded memories know as 'Q'. This may explain why they seem more informative about what He said and did. Agreement is universal that Mark is a masterly editor of oral tradition, and there is acknowledged internal and external evidence that he recorded St Peter's teaching faithfully. Where and when he completed his Gospel is uncertain. Some say this was in Rome about 65 AD, while others in Alexandria about 70 AD before the destruction of the Temple in Jerusalem. The latter opinion is based on the fact that he writes in the popular Greek then widely used in the eastern Mediterranean.

Mark's primary message is that the Good News is Jesus Christ who fulfils the prophecies, brings heaven and earth together, and whose authority to heal and to preach comes from God. Early on, he establishes Our Lord's divinity and His command over Satan who comes in the guise of demonic possession, sickness, stormy weather addressed as an evil spirit, opposition from religious leaders, and even from some disciples. The climax is reached at Caesarea Philippi when Peter hails Him as the Christ, the Son of God but is rebuked with "Get behind me Satan!" when he demurs about the rejection and suffering the Messiah must endure. Attention is drawn to the cost of discipleship and the sharing in the cup of suffering that brings mystical union with the Saviour (*cf.* 1:25, 4:39, 8:22-23).

The Kingdom of God arrives when Our Lord's ministry begins with His baptism by John in the Jordan and the heavens are torn apart, and culminates in His Passion and death when the Temple veil is similarly rent asunder. These are signs that barriers between Heaven and earth are removed by the healing power and ultimate sacrifice of the Son of God. The Transfiguration confirms Our Lord's divine Sonship, and the painful path He follows to accomplish His Father's will in the plan of salvation. The Temple must be cleansed because, like the barren fig tree, it has become fruitless. Mark concludes his Gospel with the Risen Lord's appearances, His Ascension, and His continued supportive leadership of disciples as they "proclaim the Good news to all creation" (1:10-15, 11:12-23, 15:38-39 16:9-20).

Good News of Jesus

Once considered the simplest, most historical and least theological of the four, Mark's Gospel is now appreciated differently. He uses oral and written traditions to create a deliberate pattern, and devotes a third of his text to the last week of Our Lord's life in order to share the theology of the cross with contemporary Christians already suffering persecution and expecting to die for the faith. He distinguishes Jesus as unique, the King of a realm not of this world, and so unlike the itinerant preachers and wonder-workers who were a feature of life in Palestine.

The Christians in Rome already believed that Jesus was the Messiah, the Son of God and the Saviour of Mankind, so he did not have to make a direct defence of Christianity or offer a treatise on Our Lord's earthly life. He wrote about His ministry as he learned it from listening to Peter preaching to a Gentile audience and emphasises what reveals His divinity, just as Peter did in his discourse to the household of Cornelius (*Ac* 10:34-43). His theme is " the Good News about Jesus Christ, the Son of God", and the narration shines with his own certainty of Our Lord's divinity, and the well-founded Christian belief in our Sovereign Lord. His divine Sonship is proclaimed by the Father at His Baptism and Transfiguration; demons and unclean spirits call Him "the Holy One of God", "Son of God", and Son of the Most

High God"; they fear and obey His commands; He is the Lord of the Sabbath; He demonstrates His right to forgive sin when He cures the paralytic; and He underlines this in His parable about 'The wicked Husbandmen', and in His reply to the High Priest.

Miracles

Despite its relative brevity, the Gospel records every one of Our Lord's miracles that are mentioned in the other Synoptics, and adds two more concerning the cures of the deaf man in the Decapolis region and the blind man at Bethsaida. Whether healing the sick and afflicted, controlling the forces of nature, or exercising mastery over evil spirits, Jesus is the supreme Lord of all, so that all can echo the Centurion's words on Calvary, "Indeed this Man is the Son of God" (cf. *Mk* 1:11,31, 9:7, 1:24, 3:11, 5:7, 2:10, 12:1-12, 14:62, 1:31, 2:11, 5:28, 6:56, 7:32, 8:22, 10:52, 4:39, 6:48, 1:24-27, 34, 3:11,22-27, 5:1-15, 9:16-27, 15:39; Ac 10:36).

'Abba, Father'

Mark's portrait of the divine Lord and Son of God does not obscure the human nature that He assumed at the Incarnation. He is the Incarnate Son who needs food and rest like other mortals, has compassion for the leper and the hungry crowds, is angry about the closed minds of the Pharisees, sad about the lack of faith shown by the people of Nazareth, cross with His disciples, and patiently loving towards children. His personal experience of God was paramount in His teaching and He transforms the Old Testament's formal approach when He calls Him "Abba". In Aramaic, this is the intimate and affectionate name, akin to "Daddy", that a confident and respectful child calls a parent who is entitled to obedience because he loves, protects, and makes things better. Our Lord encourages His brothers and sisters to celebrate their relationship with the Father who has created unique individuals whom He loves without limit. When we pray in times of need, danger or sorrow, He may chose not to intervene, but He has already arranged that an answer comes in the very act of turning to Him that brings realisation of the Kingdom's values. When the Son in the Garden of Gethsemane cries out in agony, "Abba, may this hour pass me by", the awful hour does indeed give way to calm submission to the Father's will, because He "came not to be ministered unto, but to minister and give His life as a redemption for many." (*Mk* 1:41, 2:10-16, 3:5, 4:38, 6:6, 8:2, 10:14-16, 45, 14:33-36).

Devotion to St Mark

"Almighty God, you chose the evangelist Saint Mark and ennobled him with the grace to preach the Gospel. Let his teaching so improve our lives that we may walk faithfully in the footsteps of Christ" (*Prayer of the Church*).

"The universal Church received the faith that it professes from the Apostles. It believes in one God, the Father almighty, the maker of heaven and earth, in Jesus Christ, the Son of God who became flesh for our salvation, and in the Holy Spirit who preached through the prophets the plans of God, the coming of our beloved Lord Jesus Christ, His Virgin birth, His Passion, Resurrection from the dead, and bodily Ascension into heaven, His return in glory to gather all things together and raise all human flesh to life so that, in accordance with the will of His Father, every knee may bow before Jesus Christ, our Lord and God, our Saviour and our King, and every tongue acknowledge Him, and all creation be subjected to His judgement" (St Irenaeus, *Office of Readings*, April 25th).

St Mark's, Venice

The winged lion of courage rather than ferocity (*Rv* 4:7) was adopted as St Mark's symbol during the fourth century. Devotion developed in Venice after the city welcomed his relics in 890 AD to prevent their being desecrated by Arabs, an event formerly commemorated with a Feast on January 31st. In St Mark's Cathedral there are twelfth and thirteenth century frescoes that depict scenes from his life, and the Venetian republic adopted his symbol, and used it widely the more prosperity increased. Venetian painters present him as saving the city from plague, as the protector of justice and law, and invariably include him in pictures of anything relating to Venice's glory. The Feast of St Mark the Evangelist in the universal Church, once September 23rd, is now April 25th. With St Luke, he is the patron of notaries.

Saint Luke

The name from the Latin Lucanus or Lucus was popular at the time and was probably given to the third Evangelist and author of the *Acts of the Apostles* when he became a freeman and full citizen of the Roman Empire. According to tradition, some internal evidence and Eusebius, he was a physician and a citizen of Antioch, the capital of Syria founded by Alexander the Great that had become the main channel of Greek culture to the East. Its location and character made it ideal for taking the Good News westward and introducing Christianity to the Greek world. Luke is thought to have been a pioneer member of the Church there, a personal follower of Our Lord and, since no other Evangelist mentions the occasion, possibly one of the two disciples to whom He revealed Himself in the breaking of bread at Emmaus in the evening of the day of the Resurrection. (cf. *Lk* 24:13-35; *Ac* 11:20).

Luke joined Paul at Troas about 50 AD, not long before the second great missionary journey, and remained his close companion and disciple until the Apostle's death some fifteen years later. Paul calls him his "beloved physician", and it is likely Luke tended his sufferings from "a thorn in the flesh" that the Fathers of the Church think might have been a distressing epileptic condition. He was Paul's faithful diarist, defended him against criticism, recorded his apostolate with care and admiration, and earned from him the tribute "fellow worker." When Paul wrote to the Corinthians he said he was sending "the brother who is famous in all the churches for spreading the Gospel as Titus' companion. More than that, he happens to be the same brother who has been elected to be our companion on this errand of mercy..." The nameless preacher is identified as Luke who is already an evangelist, working with Paul at Philippi and encouraging the Church there until they embarked together on the final return to Jerusalem.

He remained in Palestine while Paul was in prison in Caesarea, 58-60 AD, accused of violating the Temple by entering with some Greek Gentiles and consequently causing a riot. When Paul exercised his right as a Roman citizen to be tried by the imperial court, Luke accompanied him to Rome via Malta where they were shipwrecked, and stayed with him during the two years' house arrest before the case came to trial, 61-63 AD. When Paul was declared innocent, Luke supported his few remaining years of apostolic work, and during his second imprisonment in Rome, that ended with his martyrdom. Tradition has it that Luke preached in Achaia in Greece, where he may have written his Gospel, and in Boetia where he died at the age of eighty-four, like Paul a lifelong celibate (cf. *Ac* 16:10-40, 20:5; 2 *Co* 8:18; 2 *Co* 12:7; *Col* 4:14; 2 *T* 4:11).

Luke's Gospel

In style and content, Luke shows literary flair, sensitivity, and skill in Hellenist rhetoric. He may have been fortunate if Mark's framework was available, but omits *Mk* 6:45-8:26 in favour of the travel narrative of Our Lord's journey from Galilee to Jerusalem. Matthew's Gospel showed how important prayer was to Our Lord, for example after His Baptism, before appointing His Apostles, at crucial moments in His life, and during His agony in the Garden. In addition to the Lord's Prayer, Luke includes the prayers of praise like those of Our Lady, Zechariah, and Simeon that reveal the essential nature of prayer in the lives of those who follow the Master. He attaches great significance to the all-encompassing embrace of God's plan that is demonstrated by tracing Our Lord's ancestry as far back as Adam, the father of the whole human race, and the continued action of the Holy Spirit in the life of Him who begins His ministry "filled with the power of the Spirit", and brings with Him the immediacy of salvation (cf. *Is* 61:1-2; *Lk* 2:22-28, 3:21-22, 4:14, 21, 6:12, 11:1-4).

The historical quality of Luke's narrative with portraiture and recorded incidents, underlines the eminent status of Jerusalem where the Church's mission to evangelise all nations began after Pentecost (*Ac* 2). He was no longer in Palestine and wanted Christianity to be

accepted in the wider Gentile world, especially the
Roman Empire that he holds responsible for the
Crucifixion. He expresses Our Lord's concern for
vulnerable members of society, children, women, the
poor, afflicted, oppressed, disenfranchised, sinners, and
outcasts; His gentle patience when Apostles fail to
understand, the action of the Holy Spirit from the
Incarnation to Pentecost, and His continued, protective
guidance of the Church. Life for women in the society of
the day was harsh, but in this Gospel they are most
honoured in the persons of Mary the Mother of God,
Elizabeth her cousin and mother of John the Baptist, the
widow of Nairn, the woman who was a sinner, the woman
in the crowd who blesses His Mother, Mary Magdalene,
and all the courageous women who faithfully assisted and
followed Him from the start of His ministry.

For Gentiles

As well as Israel, a Gentile audience would have been
particularly comforted by the Virgin birth of the Saviour
of the whole world, and the detail of Luke's account may
have depended on the help of Mary herself. He is the only
Evangelist to record the Annunciation, the Visitation, the
scripture section of the "Hail Mary", the Magnificat, the
Presentation, and the finding of the Child Jesus in the
Temple. The Infancy narrative clearly reveals Mary's
participation in the mystery of humanity's Redemption

that culminates in her presence with the Apostles when the Church is founded at Pentecost. Similarly consoling to Gentiles is the boundless, divine compassion expressed in the moving parables of the Good Samaritan and the Prodigal Son, Our Lord's defence of the forgiven woman who washes His feet with her tears, His gentle words to the women of Jerusalem as He struggled with the Cross to Calvary, and His beatific promise to the repentant thief crucified next to Him. All can be assured that Our Lord is always at the side of the sinner who wants to return to God's mercy (e.g. *Lk* 1-2, 7:37, 8:1-3, *Ac* 1:14).

The Acts of the Apostles

As in his Gospel, Luke's writes the prologue to the *Acts* in classical, idiomatic Greek, but strikes a more familiar tone when telling a story in the style of the Septuagint version of the Scriptures to which the Jews living in the provinces were accustomed. He links sacred and secular history with observations that have been verified by modern archaeologists, and traces the progression of Christianity from Jerusalem into the Gentile world, especially to the heart of the Roman Empire. The account of how the Apostles shared all things in common and provided for the poor from the common fund shows the understanding that following Jesus involves a detachment from material things.

Some have suggested that a good alternative title would be "How the Good news came from Jerusalem to Rome",

46

the one city symbolizing the history of Israel and the
birthplace of Christianity, and the other the wider world
and the universality of Christianity. St Irenaeus, St Cyril of
Alexandria, and Tertullian regard the *Acts* as divinely
inspired scripture, and believe the writer was present at the
events described. As Luke explains to Theophilus, the Acts
are a continuation of "my earlier work" that dealt "with
everything Jesus had done and taught from the beginning
until the day he gave instructions to the apostles He had
chosen through the Holy Spirit and was taken up to
heaven." Style, grammar and vocabulary all point to the
works as coming from the same pen. 'Theophilus',
'beloved of God', might have been a sympathetic Roman
official, a convert to Christianity, or simply a fictitious
person representing all Gentile Christians who are going
to hear about the spread of Faith after Our Lord's physical
departure (cf. *Ac* 1:1-4).

Luke writes the first part of the *Acts* in the third
person, as an historian recording facts. Then, in Acts
16:10, "they" becomes "we" as the missionary journeys
are described by an eyewitness who is with Paul until
they return to Jerusalem together at the end of the third
mission. St Jerome thinks he finished writing the *Acts*
towards the end of Paul's house arrest in Rome since
there are no signs of the persecution to come, and no
mention of Paul's eventual martyrdom, or the fall of
Jerusalem (cf. *Ac* 16:10-17, 20:5-15, 21; 1-18, 27, 28:16).

Key themes and doctrinal content of Acts

- Blessed Trinity (1:4, 2:33, 8:39, 16:7).
- God the Father's Divine Plan and providence (4:27-28, 14:15-17).
- The Christian mission to bear witness to Jesus Christ, the Son of God, Messiah and divine Lord who undertakes the work of salvation (e.g. 1:8, 2:21, 47).
- The Holy Spirit who bestows His gifts of empowerment (92:28-39, 10:44-48).
- The Sacraments and Sanctifying Grace (1:5, 2:42-46, 11:30-35, 20:7).
- Liturgy and Prayer (2:46, 3:1, 6:6, 13:2-3, 14:22).
- Christianity: a movement composed of Jews and Gentiles united in fulfilling God's purpose for Israel (15:14-17, 28:20).
- The Church: a society effectively administered by Apostles, deacons and elders (2:32, 4:20, 5:30-32,6:2, 10:39, 14:23).
- The common life (2:42-47, 4:24-35, 13:52).
- The primacy of Peter (5:15, 9:38).
- The nature of miraculous events (5:15, 10:10-14).
- Christianity's triumph over magic (13:4-12, 19:13-20).

Devotion to St Luke

"Father, you chose Luke the Evangelist to reveal by preaching and writing the mystery of your love for the poor. Unite in one heart and spirit all who glory in your name, and let all nations come to see your salvation" (*Prayer of the Church*).

"The Lord follows in the wake of those who preach Him since preaching paves the way, and then the Lord Himself comes to make His dwelling-place in our hearts... Pray that the Lord of the harvest send labourers into His harvest. There are only a few labourers for a harvest so plentiful; there are many who wish to hear the Good News but few to tell it to them" (Pope St Gregory the Great, *Office of Readings*, October 18th).

Not surprisingly, doctors and surgeons have adopted St Luke as their patron who, in early art, is seen writing at his desk. Artists, too, impressed by his beautiful word-pictures seek his protection, and the tradition that he painted an icon of the Most Blessed Virgin is used by Flemish painters of the 15th and 16th centuries who depict him engaged in this task. His symbol of the winged ox (*Rv* 4:7), or sometimes a calf evoked by his Gospel's early mention of Temple sacrifices, has led butchers to place themselves under his patronage, and brewers because, as a physician, he would have been able to identify herbs and other ingredients to make and prescribe soothing or stimulating potions. There is uncertainty about his final resting place. Some say his relics were taken to Thebes and later to Constantinople in the mid 4th century, though Padua also lays claim to them, or at least a part of the treasured remains. The Feast of Saint Luke the Evangelist is October 18th.

Saint John

John and elder brother James were the sons of Zebedee and Salome who was related to Our Lord's Mother Mary. In their teens they became disciples of John the Baptist, a splendid preparation for following Jesus. Like Peter and his brother Andrew, they came from Bethsaida and probably belonged to the same fishing co-operative which shared the boat, equipment, and maintenance costs. John and Andrew became Jesus' first disciples and recruited their brothers James and Peter. Our Lord then extended an invitation to Philip who brought along Nathanael and, three days later they all accompanied Him to the marriage feast at Cana in Galilee where they witnessed His first miracle when He transformed water into wine.

Fishers of men

The new disciples stayed with Our Lord until Passover and then returned to earning their living from the sea while regularly learning from their new Rabbi. One morning towards the end of the first year of His public life, He found John with Peter, Andrew and James at the lakeside unravelling their nets. They had been fishing all night, usually the best time, but had caught nothing. He stepped into one of the boats moored at the water's edge so that the crowd following Him could see and hear more easily. When He finished speaking, He suggested that they return to deep water and try again, and it says much about the trusting relationship already established that, despite misgivings, expert fishermen took the advice of a carpenter, and were rewarded with a catch so huge that the nets were filled to breaking point.

This result deeply impressed people who saw such command over the sea and its inhabitants as a sign of divine authority. Peter fell to his knees and begged, "Leave me Lord; I am a sinful man." His own nocturnal effort had been fruitless but, with a word from Jesus, and not for the only time, sterility became abundance, His fullness from which all receive. Like Isaiah when asked by God to be His messenger to the people, Peter was painfully conscious of unworthiness before divine holiness, and acknowledged his frailty with the humility that opens the mind to the understanding of God's purposes. Jesus told him not to be afraid and that in future they would be "fishers of men" and draw all people to Him in the Gospel net. In the instant change of heart that begins the journey to God's kingdom, without a word they left their valuable boat, nets, homes and livelihood to follow Him. Experienced survivors like fishermen do not leave everything to follow a loser, or a leader who does not know where he is going. Their decision indicates the enormous impact Jesus has on those who know Him. So dynamic is His personality that demanding crowds wanted to be with Him, and even when He was worn out by his journeys, they confidently expected Him to solve all their problems (cf. *Mt* 4:18-22, 22: 34-40; *Mk* 1:16-20, 12:28-34; *Lk* 5:1-11; *Jn* 2:1).

The inner circle

Among the Twelve Apostles whom Jesus appointed, John, with Peter and James formed an elite group who would be with Him on three occasions that would demonstrate the importance of unwavering faith in Him. The first was when the young daughter of Jairus fell desperately ill. He was an elder in the synagogue at Capernaum who knew Jesus well, had heard Him preach, and had witnessed His miracles. It was natural that he should turn to Him for help but, even as he spoke, word was brought that she had died. Jesus took Peter, James and John into the house where they saw Him restore the child to life. St Mark's account retains His "Tulitha Kumi" ("Little lamb get up"), a phrase of gentle solicitude. He imposed silence on the witnesses of the miracle because the time had not come for the fulfilment of His intention that "there is nothing hidden but it must be disclosed, nothing kept secret except to be brought to light."

Six days after Peter's inspired act of faith in Our Lord as Messiah at Caesarea Philippi, He took the three to Mount

Tabor, familiar territory only a few miles from Nazareth. On this high ground He revealed to them His glorious divinity that shone with the majesty of the Lord of Creation and head of redeemed humanity. They saw Him talk to Moses and Elijah about what must be accomplished in Jerusalem to advance the plan of salvation. Peter thought the wondrous vision might herald a victorious Messianic reign, and that Moses and Elijah had returned to enjoy the triumph. In his euphoria, he said it was just as well the trio were on hand because they could improvise three shelters for Jesus and His visitors from trees at the summit.

There was no need for earthly accommodation but Peter's considerate, though impractical offer paved the way for a further revelation about the nature of the Trinity. At Jesus' baptism, the Holy Spirit had appeared as a dove, and the Father had announced, "You are my beloved Son, in whom I am well pleased." Now, at this marvellous transfiguration on Tabor, the cloud of divine presence envelopes the three Apostles, and they hear the Father's voice confirm Peter's decisive acknowledgement "You are the Christ, the Son of the Living God," with "This is my beloved Son. Listen to all He says." The vision passed and, once again, He was their familiar Master and friend. The third and final occasion would be in twelve months time when they would be with Our Lord in the garden of Gethsemane just before His arrest (cf. *Mt* 10:1-7; *Lk* 6:12-16).

John became so protective of Our Lord's honour that he tried to stop a Jewish exorcist using His name when casting out the "demons" of painful personality disorders. Both he and James showed a fierce streak when they asked Him to call fire down from heaven to consume the inhospitable Samaritans, so it is not surprising that He affectionately nicknamed them "Boanerges", "sons of thunder" (cf. *Mt* 27:56; *Mk* 1:16-20, 9:35, 15:40; *Lk* 9:54; *Jn* 1:35-39).

Ready to drink this cup

On His final journey to Jerusalem, Our Lord gives the Apostles further details about imminent events. He would be mocked and scourged, and then the Sanhedrin would engineer a death sentence that the Romans would carry out. He reassures them that this is not an inglorious end because the Messiah, who goes to His death consciously and freely, will rise again on the third day. As yet, they do not fully understand, and John and James, still hoping for positions in the Kingdom, ask their mother to approach Jesus on their behalf. Salome does so with the confidence of a family member, but with profound reverence for Him and the spiritual element of His Kingdom. Nevertheless, like most Jews, she still expected the revival of Israel as a religious state and, if honours were available, she wanted the first and second rank for her boys. In fairness, it must be remembered that she was one of the loyal band of

Galilean women who followed Our Lord unflinchingly wherever His ministry took Him. With His mother Mary and her own son John, she would be on Calvary to the bitter end, and her other son James would be the first Apostle to die for Christ.

Our Lord told her she did not realise what she was asking but, as always, when correcting false impressions under which disciples might labour, He shows none of the indignation He reserves for the subtle machinations of the Pharisees. He asked John and James if they were prepared to drink His "cup", the Hebrew metaphor of mystical union in a destiny either wonderful or disastrous, and if they would be witnesses to his work of Redemption. The total commitment they profess is the more creditable since it requires a leap of faith in the darkness of not quite understanding what He was talking about. Full comprehension would come later, when they would drink His cup to the dregs, and give their lives for the Faith.

Jesus explained that distributing honours in His Kingdom was His Father's prerogative, but other Apostles still harboured a hope that an earthly Messiah would defeat Israel's enemies and restore her leadership of the nations. They were just as ambitious as John and James, and annoyed by their attempt to secure preferment. Jesus told them their anger, born of a desire for power, was as alien to His Kingdom on earth as their colleagues' expectations. Rank has a place in His Kingdom but it is used in the selfless service of others. Whoever wants to be first must have childlike trust in the Father, and put himself as the servant of all. He is their model Servant who, by nature and by choice, reverses personal interest and gives His life in ransom for many (cf. *Ac* 12:2; *Mt* 20:17-28; *Mk* 9:30-37).

The Last Supper

In the Old Covenant, the Passover Meal celebrates the love and mercy of God the Father who delivers His chosen people from Egyptian slavery in anticipation of mankind's redemption. It recalls the sacrifice of the innocent lamb that was eaten with unleavened bread, and whose blood was sprinkled on the doorposts of Hebrew dwellings so that the avenging angel would "pass over" their homes and avert the destroying plague. The Lamb of God longed to share this last Passover with His disciples because it would be the prologue to the perfect sacrifice that secures human redemption, restores the Covenant with Israel, glorifies His Father, and is a foretaste of the heavenly banquet of God's reign. He sent John and Peter to hire an upper room from Mark's mother and organise the catering. During the meal, though conscious of His universal sovereignty, and the incomparable dignity revealed at the Transfiguration, He rises from the table and performs the lowly task of washing the disciples' feet. It is a service of charity and a lesson in humility that surpasses the ritual washing of hands. John records this service rather than the institution of the Eucharist described by the other three Evangelists because he wants us to learn from this example the attitude we should bring to participation in the Eucharist.

Our Lord tells them that no servant is greater than his master, no messenger greater than the one who sends him and, if they behave accordingly, they will experience the joy of true discipleship. The sublime moment gives way to the sad and solemn forecast of betrayal by one of His closest friends who even now sits at table with Him. Judas is already aware of his own treachery but the others are aghast that one of their tightly knit group could betray the Master to His enemies, and are confused about themselves and one another. Peter wants an end to an intolerable situation and is near enough to John to whisper "Who is it?" John leans towards Jesus with the confident familiarity of a bosom friend, "Who is it Lord?" he asks. Jesus answers by dipping a piece of bread in the oil and spice sauce and giving it to Judas sitting close by in a position of seniority.

In family communion with His Apostles, He establishes the eternal covenant and institutes the Sacrament of the Holy Eucharist, a transformed Passover in which He rids humanity of the bonds of sin and restores it to life with His Blood: "To imprint the immensity of the surpassing love He showed in His

Passion more deeply in the hearts of the faithful, He instituted this Sacrament as a perpetual memorial of His Passion. It fulfilled the type of the Old Law, was the greatest of the miracles He worked, and He left it as a unique consolation for those who were desolate at His departure." (St Thomas Aquinas, and cf. *Ex* 12:1-8, 11-14; *Lk* 22:7-13).

The Agony in the Garden

Jesus and the eleven left the house that was in Jerusalem's northwest quarter by way of the Water Gate near the Pool of Siloe. They turned north past the Temple esplanade outside Solomon's Porch, crossed the Brook Kedron ("turbid water-stream"), and went into the garden of Gethsemane ("olive-press") where vines grow alongside olives and figs, and where the pruning of the New Vine is about to begin. This estate on the western slope of Mount Olivet was near Bethany where Martha, Mary and Lazarus lived. It probably belonged to another friend and provided such a regular retreat for Jesus that Judas was confident he would find Him there when he brought the arresting party of soldiers, Levitical priests and servants of the chief priests.

Our Lord's humanity began to dread what lay in store, and He took John, Peter, and James some little distance from the others so that they could keep supportive watch while He prayed to His Father. The hour of suffering had come and His human nature recoiled from the fearsome burden of sin that He must shoulder and expiate. He was racked with anguish not only at the prospect of crucifixion, but by His own people's callous rejection, the inconstancy of friends, and the ingratitude of humanity. Beads of perspiration became drops of blood, a physical phenomenon brought on by intense fear and mental torment. In His distress, He paced back and forth three times, longing for companionable comfort but, despite their earlier protestations of reliability, the elite trio was asleep. With disappointment, isolation and, after a cry to His Father, came calm resignation, and His reproach was gentle. "Could you not have watched just an hour with me?" He had warned them to be watchful, to sustain good intentions with vigilant prayer, and resist the devil's temptations by steadfast loyalty to Christ (cf. *Mt* 26:36-56; *Mk* 13:33-37, 14:32-42; *Lk* 22:31-46; *Jn* 15-19; 1 *P* 5:8-11).

In Our Lord's company, Peter was fearless and, when Judas arrived with the arresting party, he immediately drew his sword and cut off the ear of Malchus, a servant of the high priest. Despite overwhelming odds, he was so obviously ready for a fight that Jesus had to tell him to sheath his weapon. That he was not killed on the spot, or at least arrested, was thanks to Our Lord's intervention of miraculously re-uniting the servant with his ear. However, as soon as Jesus was led captive to the palace of Caiaphas the high priest, the Apostles vanished, though Peter did at least follow at some distance to keep sight of Him. John knew Caiaphas and it seems used his influence to get Peter into the palace courtyard.

"Son, this is your Mother"

Society did not care much for childless widows and as Our Lord hung in agony on the Cross He entrusted his Mother to the care of John who was still standing bravely with her on Calvary. He accepted the guardianship of Mary who, in her turn, became the trustee of her Son's Church until Pentecost and, in John's person, accepted the human race as her children, each one a brother and sister to her own Son. In this harrowing moment both won the palm of martyrdom.

The Resurrection

Before dawn on the Sunday morning, Mary Magdalene went to the tomb ahead of the other women who were going to embalm Our Lord's body. When she saw the huge stone rolled back from the entrance and the sepulchre empty, she ran to Peter and John to tell them the Lord was not there, and she did not know where He had been taken. The two Apostles ran to the spot, the youthful John outstripping his senior. He looked through the low opening and saw the linen cloths lying on the ground, but did not go in, waiting respectfully for Peter who entered immediately. He was puzzled by what he saw because body snatchers do not remove linen bands carefully before escaping with their booty. Far from being in a confused heap, these were lying neatly where the body had been, and the napkin that had covered the head was neatly rolled up. When John went in, the light of faith dawned and he saw the truth of the Scriptures that Christ would rise from the dead.

The Apostles remained in Jerusalem until the end of Paschal Week and, once they knew that no harm could come to Jesus, they returned to their homes and occupations in Galilee. One morning, Peter, James, John, Nathanael, Thomas, and two others who had returned to the fishing business, were approaching their moorings at Capernaum after another unsuccessful night. They spotted a man on the shore about a hundred yards away but could not distinguish who it was in the early mist. He called to them in the friendliest way, "Boys! Have you caught anything to eat?" (cf. Latin Vulgate's "pueri,"/ "lads, boys"). Still irritated by failure, they were in no mood for jolly exchanges, and replied with a surly "No". The figure suggested they try again on the starboard side, but the vessel was now heading south, close to the western shore that was the unlikeliest place for a catch. Perhaps memories of the earlier miraculous draught began to stir. They dropped the nets and the result was a magnificent haul of one hundred and fifty-three fish. The detail is important because the ancient world believed this to be the precise number of all known species of fish, so it indicates the universal love of God and His Church who does not leave a single person outside her embrace. John was first to recognise that the figure was the Risen Lord (cf. *Jn* 13:21-30; 20:4-5; 21:1-19).

After the Ascension and the house at Ephesus

Early chapters of the *'Acts of the Apostles'* indicate John's close friendship with Peter and his collaboration in the administration of the infant Church. He was with him when he cured the crippled man at the Beautiful Gate and preached in the Temple, he was arrested with him by order of the priests and Sadducees and hauled before the Sanhedrin for interrogation, and went with him to Samaria to support the converts still waiting for the coming of the Holy Spirit. He did not share Peter's imprisonment, and is not mentioned again until 49 AD, when he attended the first Council of Jerusalem and is described by Paul as being "among these leaders, these pillars of the Church" (cf. *Ac* 3:1; 8:14-25; *Ga* 2:9).

When Paul was in Rome for his trial about 59 AD, John continued the mission in Ephesus. St Irenaeus of Lyons and Eusebius describe his apostolate in this Christian centre, and refer to the testimony of Polycarp and Papias, the prominent elders who link the Apostles to the early Fathers. St Polycarp, one of John's first disciples and first Bishop of Smyrna, wrote a *'Letter to the Philippians'* that endorsed the accuracy of the New

Testament, and St Irenaeus and the historian Polycrates of Ephesus agree with Polycarp, that John spent many fruitful years in Asia where Papias was a bishop.

According to Tertullian, "For having preached God's word and witnessed for Jesus", the emperor Domitian condemned John to be executed by being plunged into a cauldron of boiling oil. Miraculously, he emerged unscathed but, like his fellow Apostles, suffered all the pains of martyrdom. The Romans then banished him to the island of Patmos in the Aegean Sea where he recorded his visions in the *Book of Revelation* (cf. *Rv* 1:9), returning to Ephesus when the more congenial Nerva became emperor. The Syrian chronicler, Elia Bar Sinja, reports his peaceful death there at the age of ninety-four, and his burial on a hillside outside the city in the sixth year of Trajan's reign. A basilica was built over the tomb, and Saints Augustine, Ephrem and Gregory of Tours agree that it became a centre of great devotion and famous for miracles.

Mary's house

In his Gospel, John tells us that from the moment when the dying Jesus entrusted His mother to his care, he made a place for her in his own home. There is a tradition that when he went to Ephesus he took Mary with him and built a house where she ended her days on earth in prayer and, no doubt, adding her own recollections to his writing.

In an age when churches were built to venerate a person where they had lived, it is significant that the first known church dedicated to the Blessed Virgin was at Ephesus. In 1881, a French priest Father Julien Gouyet, discovered a book that recounted the visions of the German nun and stigmatic Blessed Anne Catherine Emerich who had died in 1824. She described the location of the inconspicuous Ephesus house where Mary lived before being taken up to Heaven. Following Sister Anne's directions, Father Gouyet found the remains of the house and reported his discovery to the Vatican.

There was cautious silence for ten years until the Lazarist Fathers in Smyrna, near Ephesus, investigated further, and their examination of the site confirmed the accuracy of the vision's details and corroborated the story of Mary's final years. They also met a local Greek community who were convinced that this was Mary's holy place, and made a pilgrimage there every year on August 15th. On this day the Eastern Church has celebrated the Feast of Mary's Dormition ("going to sleep") from the fifth century, anticipating the West's honouring her Assumption, body and soul into Heaven, on the same date.

An enquiry commissioned by the Archbishop of Smyrna concluded that the ruins were those of the house in which Mary had lived and, in 1896, Pope Leo XIII authorised pilgrimages to which his successor, St Pius X, attached a plenary indulgence. Two world wars interrupted travel and interest, but a revival followed Pope Pius XII's declaration of the Dogma of the Assumption as an article of faith in 1950, when he also declared Mary's House at Ephesus an official shrine. The number of pilgrimages grew with the encouragement of Blessed Pope John XXIII who, for the Feast of Candlemas, February 2nd 1960, sent a special candle to the restored house as a symbol of this Marian shrine's importance.

In 1967, Pope Paul VI showed his personal approval with a visit, and took a bronze lamp as "a present for the Blessed Virgin". In 1979, the first year of his Papacy, Pope John Paul II celebrated Mass there for the thousands attracted by his visit. Nowadays, pilgrims from all over the world go to the house of Mary and John, many of them Muslims in whose Koran Mary appears as the peerless model of all women. The belief that the spring beneath the building has healing properties is supported by the discarded physical aids and votive offerings left in thanksgiving, but the greatest miracle is that differing faiths gather here to honour the Mother of God.

John's Gospel

Knowing his readers were familiar with the events of Christ's life from the Synoptic Gospels of Matthew, Mark and Luke, John was able to write in a more meditative style and concentrate on the deeper significance of what

Our Lord said and did. To the Synoptics' anticipation of His second coming in glory to judge the world at the end of time, and the fulfilled perfection of the Kingdom, he adds a reflection on the mystery of the Incarnation and the revelation of Christ's glory, here and now, when judgement is at work in each individual soul. He speaks of eternal life already possessed by those who have faith, and emphasises God's victory over evil and the world's salvation that is already guaranteed by the Resurrection. He draws particular attention to God's glory and majesty made visible to the world in the person of Jesus Christ who possesses both divine and human natures.

This "spiritual" fourth Gospel records Our Lord's "I am" sayings: the Bread of Life; the Light of the World; the Gate of the Sheepfold; the Good Shepherd; the Resurrection and the Life; the Way, the Truth and the Life; the True Vine. These are metaphors associated with salvation and, all the while, John shows Him in control of His destiny, not at the mercy of His enemies. Charity is given pre-eminence as the supreme bond of love between the Father and the Son from which the Holy Spirit proceeds, the "agape" at the heart of Our Lord's injunction to love, even one's enemies, that finds sublime expression in the Sacrament of the Eucharist in which divine and human love is shared. It is a love that drives out fear so that human failings do not impose limits on hope, obscure the vision of God's glory, or take away joy in His boundless and merciful love. "Let us love one another since love comes from God and everyone who loves is begotten by God and knows God... His love for us was revealed when He sent into the world His only Son so that we could have life though him..." (1 *Jn* 4:7-10 and cf. Encyclical *'God is Love'*, Pope Benedict XVI, 2005).

The Letters of John

John's three Letters resonate the style and doctrine of his Gospel, and have a recurring theme of certainty in the light and love of God. There is warm concern for recipients who are greeted as "dear children" and "dear friends", and with the authority of one who has courageously accepted great responsibility. The first, written to the churches in Asia, summarises his religious experiences, and develops the Gospel themes to encourage the communities who have become endangered by early heresies. Saint Augustine observes John's unique appreciation of the mystery of Our Lord's life and mission: "'That which was from the beginning, which we have heard, which we have seen with our eyes, which we have looked upon and touched with our hands, concerning the word of life...' Who could touch the Word with his hands, were it not that the Word became flesh and dwelt among us? This Word who became flesh in order that He could be touched by hands, began to be flesh in the Virgin Mary's womb. But he did not then begin to be the Word,

for St John says, 'That which was from the beginning.'
See how his letter corroborates his Gospel, 'In the
beginning was the Word and the Word was with God.'" (St
Augustine, *'Commentary on the First Letter of St John'*).
Two more short letters reaffirm the law of love, and the
reality of the Incarnation in the face of doubt and denial.
John warns against those who refuse to admit that "Christ
has come in the flesh and who do the work of the
deceiving Antichrist, advises how to banish rivalries in the
community, and commends good example.

The Book of Revelation

"This is the revelation given by God to Jesus Christ about
the things that are now to take place; He sent His angel to
make it known to His servant John who has written down
everything... From John to the seven churches of Asia:
grace and peace to you from Him who is, who was, and
who is to come" (*Rv* 1:1-44)

St Irenaeus calculates that John wrote this long letter
while in exile on Patmos towards the end of Domitian's
reign, 81-96 AD. It belongs to the body of ancient
apocalyptic literature in which a visionary is entrusted
with unveiling truths that open minds to other worlds and
events, in John's case the Heavens and the end of time.
He makes his revelation to the seven churches of Asia,
then a Roman province with a thriving Christian
community. There would have been more than seven

churches so he is probably addressing seven centres of communication, or using the number in the Hebrew sense of perfect completion to speak to all God's children.

Meaning

John does not actually quote from Scripture but uses graphic Old Testament imagery from Genesis, Exodus, the Psalms, the Prophets, especially Daniel, to illustrate the fulfilment of the promises in Israel's history, and draw attention to Rome in the guise of the old enemy Babylon, and the fall of the empire. A sacrificial lamb with seven horns and seven eyes represents Our Lord, the Paschal Lamb whose single perfect sacrifice, once and for all, expiates the sins of all. The "beast" symbolizes the Antichrist, "the mystery of iniquity in the form of the supreme religious deception that offers an apparent solution to humanity's problems at the price of apostasy from the truth, a pseudo-messianism by which man glorifies himself in place of God and His Messiah who has come in the flesh" (*Catechism of the Catholic Church*, 675).

While time exists, the war against Satan continues to be waged, but God's ultimate victory is certain. Meanwhile, lessons are learnt from Israel's "fornication with other nations and their false gods. The crises of war, death and famine are envisioned, but the rainbow around God's throne signifies that He has not forgotten His promise to Noah. Finally, the transformation of a violent, threatening Lion of Juda into the Sacrificial Lamb is a profoundly appropriate conclusion to the New Testament (cf. *Rv* 21:22-23).

Devotion to St John

"Almighty God, who through your Apostle John unlocked for us the hidden treasures of your Word, grant that we may grasp with fuller understanding the message he so admirably proclaimed" (*Prayer of the Church*).

"We honour John, the Apostle who lent on the Lord's breast during the Last Supper. He drank the streams of the Gospel from their very source, the sacred breast of the Lord. Great is his happiness, to whom the secrets of Heaven have been revealed" (*Divine Office*, December 27th).

"As St John says, 'Do not bestow your love upon the world, or on what the world has to offer.' The lover of this world has no love of the Father in him. What does the world offer? Only gratification of corrupt nature, of the eye, the empty pomp of living; these things take their being from the world, not from the Father. The world and its gratification pass away" (St John Baptist De La Salle; cf.1 *Jn* 215-17).

In art, John's emblems include a book, an eagle (*Rv* 4:7) representing the soaring and meditative spirituality of his Gospel, and a cup in which a viper nests, a reminder of a challenge issued to him by the high priest of Diana at Ephesus to drink a poisoned chalice. His image is on St Cuthbert's stole embroidered at Winchester in the 9th century, and a copy of his Gospel first placed in Cuthbert's tomb is now in the British Library. Hundreds of churches have been dedicated to him and his frequent appearance on rood screens is evidence of popular appeal in the middle ages. Until the revision of the Roman calendar in 1970, his living martyrdom in the boiling oil was remembered on May 6th, Feast of Saint John before the Latin Gate. This also commemorates the dedication of the Basilica of Saint John Lateran, the highest ranking Catholic church, and episcopal seat of the Pope as Bishop of Rome. The universal Church celebrates the Feast of St John, Apostle and Evangelist, on December 27th, appropriately close to Our Lord's birthday, when white vestments are worn rather then the red of martyrs. He is the patron saint of theologians, writers and publishers.

Informative Catholic Reading

We hope that you have enjoyed reading this booklet.

If you would like to find out more about CTS booklets - we'll send you our free information pack and catalogue.

Please send us your details:

Name ....

Address ....

....

....

Postcode ....

Telephone ....

Email ....

Send to: CTS, 40-46 Harleyford Road,
            Vauxhall, London
            SE11 5AY

Tel: 020 7640 0042
Fax: 020 7640 0046
Email: info@cts-online.org.uk